Growing Up
AROUND THE WORLD

Growing Up in Australia

Other titles in the *Growing Up Around the World* series include:

Growing Up in Brazil
Growing Up in Canada
Growing Up in China
Growing Up in France
Growing Up in Germany
Growing Up in India
Growing Up in Iran
Growing Up in Italy
Growing Up in Japan
Growing Up in Mexico
Growing Up in Russia
Growing Up in Saudi Arabia

Growing Up
AROUND THE WORLD

Growing Up in Australia

Martin Gitlin

ReferencePoint Press®

San Diego, CA

Printed in the United States

For more information, contact:
ReferencePoint Press, Inc.
PO Box 27779
San Diego, CA 92198
www. ReferencePointPress.com

LIBRARY OF CONGRESS CATALOGING-IN-PUBLICATION DATA

Name: Gitlin, Martin, author.
Title: Growing Up in Australia/by Martin Gitlin.
Description: San Diego, CA: ReferencePoint Press, Inc., [2018] | Series: Growing Up Around the World | Includes bibliographical references and index.
Identifiers: LCCN 2017042514 (print) | LCCN 2017048334 (ebook) | ISBN 9781682823200 (eBook) | ISBN 9781682823194 (hardback)
Subjects: LCSH: Youth—Australia—Social life and customs—Juvenile literature. | Australia—Social life and customs—Juvenile literature. | Australia—Social conditions—Juvenile literature. | Australia—History—Juvenile literature.
Classification: LCC HQ799.A8 (ebook) | LCC HQ799.A8 G57 2018 (print) | DDC 305.2350994—dc23
LC record available at https://lccn.loc.gov/2017042514

CONTENTS

AUSTRALIA AT A GLANCE

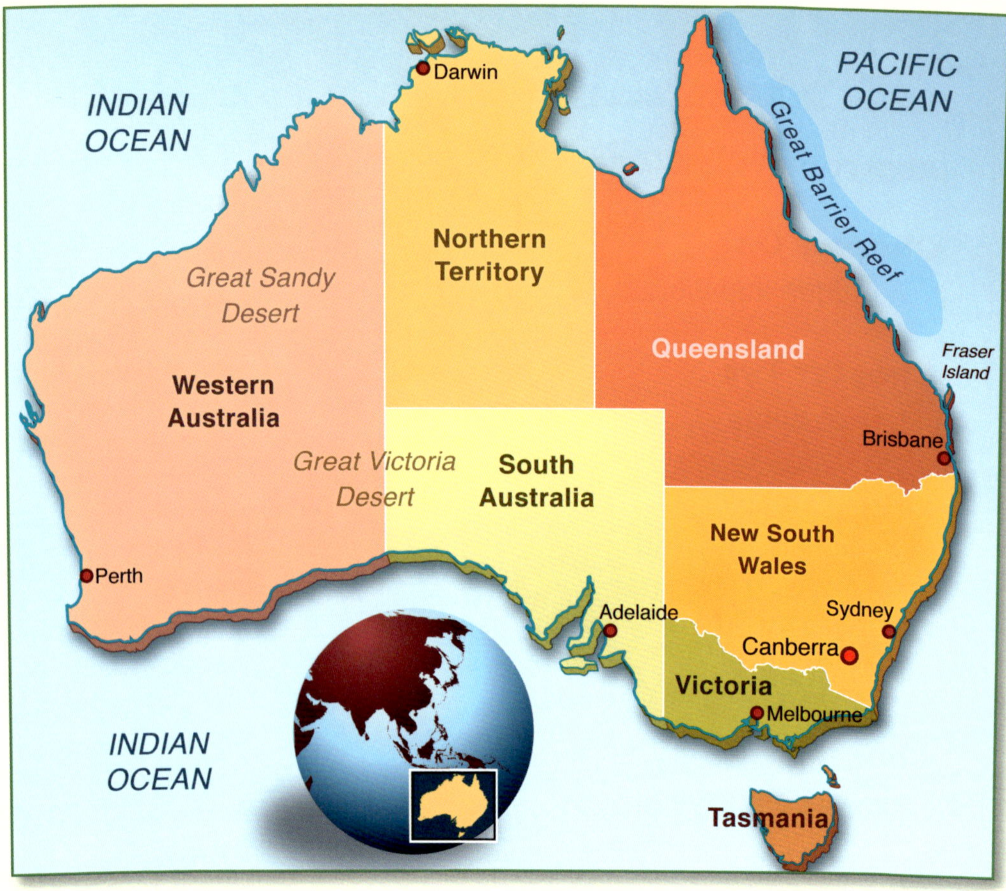

Official Name
Commonwealth of Australia

Capital
Canberra

Size
7,682,300 square miles (19,897,066 sq. km)

Total Population
22,992,654 as of 2016

Youth Population
0–14 years: 17.84%
15–24: 12.96%

Religion
Protestant: 30.1%; Catholic: 25.2%; none: 22.3%; unspecified: 9.3%; other Christian: 2.9%; Orthodox: 2.8%; Buddhist: 2.5%; Muslim: 2.2%; Hindu: 1.3%; other: 1.3%

Type of Government
Parliamentary democracy

Language
English (76.8%); all other languages (under 2%)

Currency
Australian dollar

Industries
Mining, industrial and transportation equipment, food processing, chemicals, steel

Literacy
99% (age 15+ able to read and write)

Internet Users
19.238 million, or 84.6% of population

CHAPTER ONE

A Unique and Vibrant Land

Australia is the only country in the world that takes up an entire continent. With the Pacific Ocean to its east and the Indian Ocean to its west, it is surrounded by water. It is also the world's only populated continent located entirely south of the equator. Australia boasts several other geographical distinctions. It is the largest nation located solely in the Southern Hemisphere. It is the largest island on Earth. Its average elevation is the lowest of any continent. And it is the only continent without glaciers.

Australia is also the driest continent aside from Antarctica. About 35 percent of its land mass receives so little rain that the area can be classified as a desert. In the state of Western Australia, the Great Victoria and the Great Sandy Deserts cover about 100,000 square miles (258,999 sq. km).

Not only is Australia an island, but its territory includes thousand of other islands. The most famous is Tasmania, which is located off the southeastern coast. This Australian state owes its name to Dutch explorer Abel Janszoon Tasman, who discovered the island in 1642. Tasmania boasts some of the most beautiful mountain, lake, and coastal scenery in the country. Much of its land is protected in national parks and reserves.

Fraser Island, located off the Queensland coast in the northeastern quadrant of the country, is the largest sand island in the world. Its sand hills rise to nearly 800 feet (244 m). Forty perched dune lakes dot the island, representing about half the world's total. Perched dune lakes are formed when organic matter such as leaves, bark, and dead plants gradually builds up and hardens in depressions created by wind. Fraser Island also features rain forests and extensive wildflower heaths. Its bird life is abundant, and there are also a few species of mammals, such as bats and dingoes, which are native to Australia. The southwestern part of Fraser Island is a tourist resort.

A Diverse Landscape

Australia boasts a diverse landscape. Forests cover much of the south. Huge deserts and scrubland dominate the outback region in the west. The mountains of the Great Dividing Range separate the dry interior from rain forests along the eastern coast. Tropical grasslands cover northern Australia. The corals of the Great Barrier Reef extend thousands of miles along the northeastern coast.

The term *outback* describes any inland area separated from the large population centers. It is generally applied to arid and semiarid areas of the country, including those in eastern Australia, the Western Plateau, and the northern plains in the west. Several prominent mountain ranges and the country's four main deserts are situated in the outback. Cattle have been raised on the outback's paltry vegetation in the far north, and sheep have been kept on large landholdings, called stations, since the late nineteenth century. Mining in the outback has provided natural gas and oil, but the practice has been opposed by environmentalists, including many among the youth of Australia.

The Great Barrier Reef is the longest and largest reef complex in the world, with an area of about 135,000 square miles (350,000 sq. km). It is home to three hundred species of hard coral as well as sponges, worms, lobsters, crayfish, prawns, crabs, and a large variety of fishes and birds.

The outback and the Great Barrier Reef are known for their wildlife. Some, like the iconic kangaroo and koala, are relatively mild mannered. Others have the distinction of being among the world's deadliest creatures. In his book *In a Sunburned Country*, American author Bill Bryson describes some of these dangers. He writes that Australia has more things that will kill you than anywhere else:

> Of the world's ten most poisonous snakes, all are Australian. Five of its creatures—the funnel web spider, box jellyfish, blue-ringed octopus, paralysis tick, and stonefish—are the most lethal of their type in the world. This

> is a country where even the fluffiest of caterpillars can lay you out with a toxic nip, where seashells will not just sting you but actually sometimes *go* for you. . . . If you are not stung or pronged to death in some unexpected manner, you may be fatally chomped by sharks or crocodiles, or carried helplessly out to sea by irresistible currents, or left to stagger to an unhappy death in the baking outback. It's a tough place.[1]

Despite the geographic diversity, temperatures rarely plummet to freezing. They do, however, often soar to 100°F (38°C) in the outback. Periods of heavy rain frequently occur in the north each summer and in the south during the winter.

People who live in Australia can visit and enjoy a diversity of environments. The Great Barrier Reef, pictured, is a haven for divers interested in colorful marine life.

Uluru–Kata Tjuta National Park, located in the heart of the outback, is about 1,500 miles (2,416 km) distant from the bustling coastal cities of Melbourne and Sydney and the capital city of Canberra. But it feels like light-years away in atmosphere. The remoteness of the outback and most of Australia is in stark contrast to the densely populated urban areas, nearly all of which are located on or near the southeastern and southwestern coasts.

Populous Cities

A huge majority of the Australian population can either hear the ocean through an open window in their homes or drive a short distance to swim in the waters of either the Pacific Ocean or the Indian Ocean. Forty percent of the nearly 23 million Australians reside in the coastal cities of Sydney and Melbourne alone. The five largest cities—Sydney, Melbourne, Brisbane, Perth, and Adelaide—make up nearly two-thirds of the country's total population, and each of those cities has a population exceeding 1 million people.

> "This is a country where even the fluffiest of caterpillars can lay you out with a toxic nip, where seashells will not just sting you but actually sometimes *go* for you."[1]
>
> —Bill Bryson, an American author

Sydney is perhaps the most visually enticing city in Australia. Located on the southeastern coast in New South Wales, it is the largest city in the country. Sydney boasts a breathtaking harbor that serves as one of the most important ports in the South Pacific. The contrast between the ocean and the modern, tall buildings gives the harbor a distinctive look. British travel writer Anthony Horowitz describes his visit to Australia in 2015 during the annual Vivid Festival, which, he writes, is

> an event that has to be seen to be believed. In essence, the entire city goes quite spectacularly mad with very sophisticated, computer-generated light displays projected on to major landmarks. The opera house catches fire, shimmers, flickers and explodes. Green tendrils snake out of the windows of Customs House before the entire building disintegrates into a thousand butterflies and blossoms. The new Museum of Contemporary Art—worth a visit in

itself—becomes electrified. The streets are filled with giant pigs, molecules, mazes, brilliantly illuminated trees. There were even spotlights underneath the water. As I joined the thousands of people in the cold night air, I was struck by the cheerfulness of it all, the sense of childish wonderment. It could only happen in Australia.[2]

Aussies who want to be near the cities but prefer to avoid the fast pace of city life are relocating to suburbs. Suburban communities now surround every big city. Many suburban residents commute to the cities for work. As elsewhere, suburban commuters often face congested traffic and long drive times. Morning rush-hour drives from the suburbs to the central business districts of Sydney and Melbourne are especially bad. Those drives can take anywhere from 50 percent to 70 percent longer than the same drives would take during the middle of the night, according to a 2017 report by the Grattan Institute, a public policy think tank.

Population

Growth in population could make those commutes even worse. Australia has a population of nearly 23 million. The 2016 census reveals that about 31 percent of all Australians are under the age of twenty-five. About 18 percent are aged fourteen and younger. The population of Australia is growing. The census shows the population grew by more than 2 million between 2010 and 2016. This steady rise by an average of about 360,000 per year is a reflection of several factors.

> **"As I joined the thousands of people in the cold night air, I was struck by the cheerfulness of it all, the sense of childish wonderment. It could only happen in Australia."[2]**
>
> —Anthony Horowitz, a British travel writer

One of these factors is a longer life expectancy. Australians' average life expectancy has risen to 82.8 years, ranking Australia among the top four countries for longevity, according to a survey conducted by the World Health Organization. The high marks are due to the country's strong health care system. But the statistics are not all favorable. The indigenous population, which numbers about 650,000 according to the 2016 census, lives an aver-

The Sydney Opera House becomes an artistic canvas during the annual Vivid Festival. Thousands of spectators watch as light-show artists project color patterns and moving images upon this building and other city landmarks during the celebration.

age of 10 years less than their fellow Australians due to poorer health habits and less access to medical care.

The factor that most influenced the country's population growth, particularly in the urban centers, was an influx of immigrants. The majority have come from such Asian nations as China, India, and Vietnam. Australia today is one of the most culturally diverse nations in the world. Census data published in 2017 showed that more than 6 million Australians were born abroad. That represents 26 percent of the population, a larger figure than other English-speaking countries, including the United States, Canada, and New Zealand.

These numbers illustrate a population shift taking place in Australia. Though the United Kingdom remains the most common country of birth other than Australia itself, for the first time

The Amazing Uluru

The uniqueness of Australia's geology is embodied by one of its most popular attractions. The wide-open outback is home to Uluru, otherwise known as Ayers Rock. The world's largest monolith stands 1,142 feet (348 m) high and 5.8 miles (9.3 km) in circumference.

Uluru is considered sacred to those of Aboriginal Anangu descent, who belong to a culture that extends back about sixty thousand years. They are the traditional owners and guardians of the Uluru–Kata Tjuta National Park, where Ayers Rock and over forty sacred Aboriginal sites are located. The Anangu believe that their culture has always existed in central Australia and that its landscape was created at the beginning of time by the travels of great ancestral beings. They cite Uluru as physical evidence of these ancient events. Uluru has been used for traditional ceremonies and rites of passage for more than ten thousand years.

most foreign-born residents are now from Asia rather than Europe. "This is the changing demographic face of Australia," says University of Sydney migration expert Anna Boucher. "It is consistent with a trend towards higher Asian immigration that we have seen since the 1980s with rises in skilled migration, international students, and family reunification."[3]

Census data published by the *Financial Times* reveals that of the 1.3 million immigrants who have made Australia their home since 2011, China (191,000) and India (163,000) are the most common countries of birth. The results have been dramatic. The number of Australian residents speaking languages at home other than English has risen to 27 percent, up from 23 percent in 2011. The most common are Mandarin, Arabic, and Cantonese.

Immigrant Influences

The influence of these recent immigrants is most visible in Australia's cities. Australian supermarkets and restaurants offer Chinese, Indian, and Italian food. Australians of all cultural backgrounds have become adept at using chopsticks. A growing Sudanese community in Victoria and New South Wales has created an African influence. The wave of Asian immigration has resulted in some native Australians adopting Buddhism or Hinduism as their religions of choice. Many immigrants have formed cultural centers that have attracted others into their communities, such as Chinatown districts and Italian café strips.

The presence of so many different foreign languages, foods, religions, and cultural practices has created a vibrant new mix of people and culture in Australia. Victor Dominello, the minister for citizenship and multiculturalism in New South Wales, recognizes these differences in his own state, where about four in ten people have at least one parent born overseas. As the son of two Italian immigrant parents, Dominello understands well the dynamics of retaining past cultural ties while adopting new cultural customs and values. "There is obviously a broad spectrum of views in Australia, as there is around the world, in relation to multiculturalism," Dominello says. "When we talk about multiculturalism we must frame multiculturalism within the Australian way of life—that is, within the Australian laws, within the Australian values."[4]

> **"This is the changing demographic face of Australia. It is consistent with a trend towards higher Asian immigration that we have seen since the 1980s with rises in skilled migration, international students, and family reunification."[3]**
>
> —University of Sydney migration expert Anna Boucher

The increase in Asian immigration and the resulting language barriers have not come without controversy. Political debate has swirled in Canberra and beyond about possible changes to immigration laws. One of these proposed laws would require immigrants to speak English before they can earn citizenship. Australia immigration minister Peter Dutton has even claimed that immigrants who live in communities where no English is spoken do not abide by Australian laws.

Such negativity is not embraced by Australia's young adult population, who tend to be more accepting and even embracing of multiculturalism than are older generations. A recent survey of more than twenty-five thousand Australians, including young adults aged eighteen to twenty-nine, found that this group is especially receptive to learning about the customs and heritage of immigrant groups. Eighty-five percent of survey respondents in this age group said they agree or strongly agree with the value of such learning. Although attitudes have fluctuated over the years, Australians—young and old—generally believe that immigration and multiculturalism have been good for their country. When asked about the benefits of multiculturalism, for instance, 86 percent agreed that it has been good for Australia.

Australia's Origins

Australia has a mixed history when it comes to dealing with other cultures. The country's Aboriginal population had lived on the continent for about fifty thousand years before Europeans arrived. By the seventeenth century, when Europeans began sailing along the coast, the land was already populated by about three hundred clans of hunters and gatherers, speaking 250 different languages and 700 dialects. Each clan felt a spiritual connection to the land on which they lived. Despite their ties to various areas, such as the deserts of the outback, the tropical rain forests, or the mountainous regions, all Aboriginal peoples embraced the notion of a mythical and magical force. They believed spirit ancestors forged all aspects of life during a period of world creation called Dreamtime and that they continued to connect to the past, present, and future through all aspects of Aboriginal culture. The more spiritual Aboriginal Australians remain strongly tied to these conceptions.

Aboriginal culture was firmly established when Captain James Cook claimed the land for Britain in 1770 and turned it into a penal colony eighteen years later. He chartered eleven ships carrying fifteen hundred people, half of whom were convicts, and landed in what is now Sydney Harbor. By 1868 half of the sixteen hundred men and women of British origin living in Australia were convicts serving time in the penal colony.

Aboriginal people were displaced by settlers during the late eighteenth century. Cheap and fruitful farmland attracted more British settlers, many of whom moved into Aboriginal territory. The squatters settled in areas that became modern-day Adelaide and Melbourne. The discovery of gold in New South Wales and Victoria in 1851 lured thousands of newcomers, including unsavory wealth seekers from around the world. Much of that wealth wound up in Melbourne and Sydney, which had become thriving cities by the 1880s.

A photo of Aboriginal men taken in the 1870s displays a mix of traditional artifacts and European-style clothing. Australia's Aborigines have kept strong ties to their ancestral roots even as nonnative cultures have greatly impacted their lifestyles.

Government

The six states of Australia—New South Wales, Queensland, South Australia, Tasmania, Victoria, and Western Australia—became one nation under one constitution on New Year's Day in 1901. What is officially known today as the Commonwealth of Australia is a parliamentary democracy that values the freedoms of press, expression, and religion. As in the United States, the government consists of three branches: executive, legislative, and judicial. Each branch acts as a check on the other so that no one branch gains excessive power. The executive branch consists of the prime minister and his or her cabinet. The legislative branch consists of Parliament, which includes the Senate, with 76 members, and the House of Representatives, with 150 members. Members of both houses of Parliament are subject to reelection every three years. The judiciary is represented by the High Court of Australia, which consists of seven justices. Australia also has a system of state and territorial courts that handle civil and criminal proceedings.

Australia has two major political parties. The Liberal/National Coalition is considered the more conservative of the two. The Australian Labor Party has been described as democratic socialists and is considered more left of center politically. The environmentally focused Green Party has gained popularity in recent years, particularly among the youth of Australia. The Liberal/National Coalition enjoyed a slight majority in the 2017 Parliament.

The differences between the three parties on political and social issues is significant. The Liberal/National Coalition favors min-

Anzac Day

About 18 percent of Australia's male population fought in World War I, and sixty thousand of those soldiers died. The one battle that lives on in Australia's collective memory occurred on April 25, 1915. On that date about 20,000 Australian soldiers landed on Turkey's Gallipoli peninsula. More than 700 of them were killed on that first day of fighting. At the end of the disastrous siege, 8,709 Australian soldiers had perished.

The country would never forget April 25. It became a national holiday called Anzac Day, which honors the Australian and New Zealand Army Corps that took part in the battle. Thousands of Australians pay tribute to those who died, and a commemoration is held at the Australian War Memorial in Canberra.

The fruitless fight at Gallipoli fueled antiwar sentiment in Australia. One Australian soldier who survived blamed the British government, which played a role in the decision to attack the peninsula. "It was the absurd sacrifice of young men by old men sitting in stuffed chairs in London," he said.

Quoted in Gallipoli: The Making of a Nation, "25th April 1915." www.gallipoli.net.au.

imal government involvement in the economy, generally opposes gay marriage, and is less concerned about combating climate change. The Labor Party fights for increased taxes on higher-wage earners, backs gay marriage, and battles strongly to reduce carbon emissions in their country. The Greens work toward increased business and environment-related taxes and strongly support gay marriage and the elimination of greenhouse gases that harm the environment and contribute to climate change.

Despite their political differences, members of Parliament—representing their particular parties—have worked together to adopt several initiatives based on issues of fairness. In 1984, for instance, Parliament passed a law that requires equal pay for women. And over the course of twenty-five years, Parliament dismantled the White Australia policy. This policy, adopted early in the twentieth century, essentially barred non-Europeans from immigrating to the country. The last parts of that policy were officially removed in 1973. The banishment of White Australia to the pages of history has promoted multiculturalism. It has allowed those seeking a better life to immigrate to Australia from all over the world.

That official openness is a part of the evolution of a country that is ever-changing socially and politically. That openness reflects modern Australia, as do the sprawling cities and thriving economy, all of which provides a stunning contrast to the serenity of rural Australia, a world that is filled with indigenous cultures, unique wildlife, and scenic beauty.

CHAPTER TWO

Life at Home

When his school day ends, Dylan Burke, like many other Australian teens, goes to basketball practice and then comes home to do his homework. He also spends about forty-five minutes a day perusing websites, e-mails, and Facebook. His younger brother, Aidan, is not into Facebook. He does play computer games, but only for about a half hour each day. His usual after-school routine includes walking the family dog, watching some television, and talking with his parents. "Sometimes we sit down and talk, we watch a lot of movies together, we have dinner,"[5] Aidan says.

The Burke boys, who live in Australia's capital city of Canberra, have a fairly typical home life among Australian youth. This is according to a survey of about two hundred Canberra teens. While they do use smartphones and social media, they are just as likely to engage in offline pursuits, such as spending time with family.

The research into Australian teens, which was done by the Education Institute at the University of Canberra, provides insight into their home lives. That research generally shows that most teens embrace the ideal of family togetherness. They also have strong study habits and view recreation as a path to achieving both a healthy mind and healthy body.

The report that resulted from the teen surveys was written by Karen Macpherson, who not only directed studies of young people but also conducted in-depth and random interviews with twenty students from eight schools. And Macpherson, who was already quite experienced exploring the hearts and minds of Australian teens, having raised five of her own, concluded that the stereotypical view of them glued to their laptops and other modern devices does not reflect reality. "This study suggested that young people today spend most of their time doing what they have done after school for generations; spending time with family, playing sport[s], doing jobs around the house; and doing homework—albeit with high use of the internet for research."[6]

Modern Families

Though such reports indicate that Australian teens most often commit themselves to the same pursuits undertaken by those of generations past, much has changed in the circumstances surrounding their home lives. Of the 30 percent of all Australians who are twenty-four or younger, the majority live in traditional two-parent households. However, in recent years many young people have grown up in nontraditional families. Families headed by same-sex couples, for instance, are becoming more common in Australia. The number of such families increased 72 percent during the first decade of the 2000s, resulting in more children than ever living with gay parents.

> "Young people today spend most of their time doing what they have done after school for generations; spending time with family, playing sport, doing jobs around the house; and doing homework."[6]
>
> —Karen Macpherson, University of Canberra researcher

There is also greater multiculturalism experienced in the homes of Australian teens, which has led to an increased number of families in which several generations live under one roof. The 2016 census showed that half of all Australians have at least one parent born overseas and that such multicultural families are more likely to embrace customs particular to their countries of birth. Among them is the embracing of extended families inside the home.

Some of Australia's young people grow up in families with a single parent, with unmarried mothers and fathers, or as part of blended families with remarried parents. Although divorce rates have stabilized and even shrunk a bit in recent decades, about one in three marriages still end in divorce. That has affected the lifestyles of young people from those families. Many of those with divorced parents no longer consider one dwelling their home. They spend significant time in the residences of both parents. Nearly half of all children of divorced parents see the parent they do not live with more than once a year, but the rest see their noncustodial parent less frequently.

The divorce rate in Australia peaked in 2001 and remained high for several years before falling. About half of the forty-seven thousand divorces averaged annually in the country between 1994 and 2014 involved families with children. The fallout from divorce takes on several forms. Children and adolescents must deal with the initial shock and find a way to recover. Some young people may feel the need to protect their siblings emotionally, and some even wrongly blame themselves for the breakup of their parents.

An Australian mother and her child feed a kangaroo at a Queensland wildlife park. The country's families have a diverse makeup, and there are many single parents who raise children on their own.

During an interview, divorce was fresh on the mind of sixteen-year-old Claudia, whose parents had split up just months earlier. Claudia experienced a period of depression during which she gained a significant amount of weight and lost her motivation before recovering. She also felt responsible for the emotional well-being of a younger sister, which resulted in a greater sense of burden. "It wasn't an easy divorce," she recalled. "I've got a little sister. She's 13-years-old and when my parents divorced I felt like I had to step up. I stepped up to be like a second mom to my sister." Claudia went on to describe the depression from which her sister was suffering and her refusal to heap the weight of that knowledge on her parents. "[Neither] of my parents knew what was going on—only I knew."[7]

> **"I've got a little sister. She's 13-years-old and when my parents divorced I felt like I had to step up. I stepped up to be like a second mom to my sister."[7]**
>
> —Sixteen-year-old Claudia

Family structure and family dynamics have a strong influence on young people's lives and upbringing. Other factors also influence youths' lives. One of these is the region of the country in which a young person grows up.

Living in the City

Many of Australia's young people grow up in an urban environment. The high cost of living in the city has motivated many families to downsize from houses to apartments. Housing prices in some parts of Sydney are similar to those in San Francisco, which has some of the highest prices in the United States. As a result, an increasing number of urban families have moved to apartment complexes. In Sydney, for instance, 41 percent of all three-bedroom units in high-rise buildings are occupied by families with kids.

Young people who grow up in urban settings like this gain life experiences that suburbanites usually do not and often have more interaction with the outside world. One of these young urbanites is the four-year-old son of Sydney mom and radio producer Nicola Harrison. She was skeptical about her move to a city apartment, but she eventually discovered its benefits for her son. "The great part of living where we do is that our little boy is a part of something," Harrison writes on the website MamaMia.

"Because we can walk everywhere, all the shop owners know him. He's showered with free bread rolls, gifts of apples, and the lovely woman who runs the café in our building rushes out with a tiny teddy whenever he walks past with me. Sometimes it can even feel too much. . . . But aside from all the attention and smiles, he is getting a behind the scenes tutorial on life."[8]

Australian journalist and photographer Elize Strydom, who has documented the lives of teenage girls in her country, writes about her experiences living in small inland and seaside towns as well as in Sydney. Time and experience have allowed her to understand the attractions of both lifestyles for Aussie youth. She recalls fantasizing about urban life as a youth living in a small town. "I remember sitting in my bedroom when I was a teenager, looking out the window and thinking, 'I'm missing out on life! There's so much life out there and I've got to wait until it's my turn to step out into this world that I know is out there.' I was so dramatic." Strydom has since been living in Sydney, but she no longer feels the same. "I am definitely very happy in the city," she reports, "but when I went back to [the seaside town of] Woolgoolga recently for three days, I was like, 'oh, this is paradise!' It's always that 'grass is greener' thing. [Seeing both sides] has certainly made me appreciate what I had growing up."[9]

Suburban Lifestyles

For many Australian youth, the city is a place to visit but not to live. Large numbers of young people grow up in the suburbs that have developed around the cities. Though they might be only 10 miles (16 km) distant from the apartments of the city, the lifestyle differences for teenagers make them feel light-years apart. A suburban home often features a lush, green backyard with trees and a nearby park with a cricket field. Young people gain a sense of privacy living in a house separated from others on the block and away from the hustle and bustle of the city.

Although the average Australian family includes two kids, the houses that they live in tend to be bigger than they once were. The typical new house built in Australia today is 30 percent bigger than it was in 1987. This has resulted in more children having their own bedrooms, but it has also meant that they interact less with their brothers and sisters. Those who seek to foster stronger relationships with parents and siblings can certainly make time to

Lighter Meals, Healthier Fare

The tradition of Australian teenagers joining their parents at the dinner table has not ended. But such occasions have become far less frequent. After-school activities such as jobs and sports have taken a bite out of the traditional ritual known as the family meal.

Teens are part of the trend toward eating in shifts. They depend on frozen foods or packaged dinners that require little cooking skill. Their meals, even with family members, are often consumed while fiddling with their smartphones or watching television.

Families that do dine together no longer partake in the same meat-and-potatoes dinners as in generations past. Lighter fare, such as salads, chicken, pasta, stir-fries, and vegetarian dishes, dominate the table. Ethnic influences have resulted in Australians eating more Thai, Mexican, Japanese, Italian, and Chinese food.

Though fast-food outlets such as McDonald's, KFC, Pizza Hut, and Subway have gained popularity among Australian teenagers, so has the notion of eating a healthy diet. Among those who have embraced the concept is fifteen-year-old Georgia Boonen of suburban Sydney. She rises early to create a liquid breakfast consisting of kale, banana, blueberries, and almond milk. And Boonen is not the only student at her private school drinking similarly healthful smoothies during math class. "It's become a real sort of culture at school," she explains. "Eating healthy is definitely something that's admired."

Meg Mason, "How Green Smoothies and Kale Became Cooler than Macca's," News.com.au, October 5, 2015. www.news.com.au.

spend with them. But fewer kids, larger homes, and the attraction of computers and smartphones add up to less family interaction for kids who do not take that initiative.

Life in Rural and Remote Areas

Rural life in Australia differs in many ways from urban living. Rural families tend to be larger than families living in urban and suburban areas. Rural residents, in general, also experience less stress than people living in or near cities. According to a 2017 article that cites two studies of Australian health and well-being, rural residents "tend to be less stressed, less anxious, feel safer and more connected with their communities and generally just . . . happier than those who live in the cities."[10]

But as this article and others also note, daily life in rural areas can be far more challenging than living in or near the cities. The chance that a child in rural and remote Australia will be confronted with trauma or adversity is greater than in urban and suburban areas of the country. The Trauma and Grief Network stresses that problems facing young Aussies growing up in rural and remote areas go beyond such issues as abuse, neglect, and other forms of mistreatment. Young people and families in remote areas deal with natural disasters such as drought and brushfires, greater financial hardships sometimes caused by these conditions, and overall isolation from peers. Getting help for these and other issues can be especially difficult. Such services are often limited in remote areas of the country. "There is no difference in common mental health risk factors between the city and rural or remote locations," states a 2017 report by the government agency Child Family Community Australia. Rather, the problem, the report continues, is that "rural and remote residents are at greater risk of experiencing poorer mental health because of insufficient early intervention and prevention services."[11] The result is that Australian children and teenagers in remote areas have been linked with poor mental health, higher suicide rates, and substance abuse.

> **"Rural and remote residents are at greater risk of experiencing poorer mental health because of insufficient early intervention and prevention services."[11]**
>
> —Child Family Community Australia, an agency that supports child, family, and community welfare service providers

But community development programs aimed at Aboriginal and Torres Strait Islander children and young people are attempting to address these problems. One such program, Stronger Communities for Children, strives to give these young people "the best possible start in life through safer families and communities, nurturing educational environments, positive participation opportunities and cultural events,"[12] according to the group's website. With funding from the prime minister and cabinet department, the group is working with local people to determine what services are needed, where, and how they should be provided.

No Place to Live

Efforts are also being made to help Australia's young homeless population. Sixty percent of the one hundred thousand Australians regarded as homeless are younger than thirty-five, and

A homeless man sits in front of a shop window in Sydney's commercial district. Three-fifths of Australia's homeless population is under age thirty-five.

around twenty-five thousand among the total homeless population are Aborigines and Torres Strait Islanders. There is also a disproportionately high percentage of homeless youth in the LGBTI (lesbian, gay, bisexual, transgender, intersex) community, according to the Australian Institute of Health and Welfare. Though the exact numbers are unknown, international research has proven that in countries such as the United States and England, about 25 percent of all homeless are identified as LGBTI.

Young Australians with mental illnesses are three times more likely to wind up homeless. Their prospects of positive health and social outcomes fall significantly. The charity Mission Australia expressed alarm and frustration over the risk factors that left forty-four thousand young people without a safe place to sleep,

A Different Kind of Extended Family

Aboriginal kids have mothers and fathers, sisters and brothers, just like boys and girls in other families. But the people in Aboriginal communities consider themselves part of one family that takes care of everyone else in it, including the children. It is a complex social structure in which the children are protected and, in turn, are raised to take part in the process of protecting the young when they get older.

The phrase "one community, many eyes" aptly conveys the Aboriginal philosophy on child rearing. Looking after the young and raising them to be active participants is the collective responsibility of all community members. Though each community differs a bit in how children are raised, children are highly valued in Aboriginal culture.

This system of child rearing results in a strong camaraderie and familiarity between kids and adults. They live in small communities in which everyone knows each other. "When you live in a community, you are pretty much all family," says one Aboriginal mother in the Northern Territory. "You are related some way or another or you are very close and all the kids, naturally they are going to know each other as they roam around."

Shaun Lohoar, Nick Butera, and Edita Kennedy, "Strengths of Australian Aboriginal Cultural Practices in Family Life and Child Rearing," Child Family Community Australia, CFCA Paper no. 25, 2014. https://aifs.gov.au.

according to a 2017 report. "It is unacceptable in 21st century Australia that there are so many children and young people homeless," says Mission Australia head Catherine Yeomans. "They deserve a safe home and we have the means to provide it. All that is needed is the political will and the commitment from us all as a community."[13] Those who spend a significant amount of time on the streets are much more likely to deal with depression and even contemplate suicide.

One organization that works to prevent and address homelessness is called Kids Under Cover. This organization promotes the building of small apartments in backyards to help keep young people connected to family. The organization also provides scholarships to maintain some form of education or job training for homeless youth. Its chief executive officer, Jo Swift, comments on some of the issues concerning youth homelessness in Australia: "It's just not about a roof overhead—it's about having a stable and secure place to call home, it's about having a solid foundation . . . the support, security and care they need to explore their potential and become happy, healthy, and productive members of society."[14]

Household Chores

Young Australians who are fortunate enough to live with their families do not always participate in the routines that keep most households running smoothly. Studies show that Australian youth spend little time helping around the house. Though more mothers than ever before are working outside the home and many have become the chief breadwinners in their families, they continue to do far more housework than anyone else. And they are receiving little help from their offspring. Surveys published by the Australian Bureau of Statistics (ABS) reveal that the overall input of Australian teenagers to household chores, never very high, is shrinking. The ABS report states that teenage girls are becoming more "domestically useless,"[15] catching up with their male counterparts in that dubious distinction. The research further showed that teenage boys spent just ten minutes a day doing household chores. One in three reported that they did no housework at all. Girls averaged just twenty-eight minutes of housework daily. The number of girls that did no housework had nearly tripled over a fourteen-year period.

Another ABS survey concludes that parents are taking an ineffective approach to convincing their teens to contribute to the housework and that the kids are learning the wrong lessons. "Most Australian parents justify requests for housework in terms of preparation for the future, rather than in terms of equitable division of work that must be done now," it claims. "Their skeptical offspring . . . do not consider their involvement in household chores as an opportunity to learn valuable skills (and) feel little responsibility for home chores. [They] experience parental requests . . . as harassment."[16]

The one exception to the household chore situation is the desire of many kids to have their own spending money (or pocket money, as it is known in Australia). A 2016 report by an Australian bank found that 87 percent of the country's young people earn pocket money—mostly by doing household chores. Even young children are getting into the act. A separate survey found that two out of three kids in primary grades receive pocket money—and 82 percent of those earn that money by doing chores. The top pocket money chores identified in that survey included:

- Tidying the bedroom (85%)
- Setting the dinner table or cleaning up after dinner (77%)
- Taking out the rubbish (67%)
- Looking after pets (66%)
- Cleaning the house (50%)[17]

What's more, young Aussies are not spending their pocket money as soon as they get it. Many are saving it for another day. Almost half (47 percent) of young respondents say they save their pocket money every week.

Great Explorations

Some may be saving their earnings for family vacations. Australians are generally quite adventurous when it comes to vacations. They frequently travel overseas, according to Australian journalist Kat George, who wrote in 2015 about the love of those from her native land to travel abroad. She mused that so many Aussies vacationed to other lands that she wondered who was taking care of the nation.

> "Going to Bawley Point is the quintessential summer family holiday, with the pulsing surf, hot sand between the toes and the feeling of flying back to shore in the foam of a crashing wave."[18]
>
> —Fifteen-year-old Clare Baxter

But Australian teenagers seem perfectly content to explore their own country as well. Not only do family vacations provide an ideal opportunity for bonding with parents and siblings, but they also quench a thirst for fun and adventure. Various vacation spots in Australia cater to all teen tastes. Some enjoy the pace and activity in big cities such as Sydney and Melbourne. Others prefer camping and exploring the million-acre resort known as El Questro, located in the northwestern corner of the country. Water parks and beaches also provide endless fun.

Vacationers swim in the Adelaide River in Australia's Northern Territory. The rivers, mountains, beaches, and deserts that make up the country provide both adventure and relaxation for millions of Australians.

Bawley Point in New South Wales is a favorite spot for fifteen-year-old Clare Baxter. Her family avoids the crowds of the cities and instead travels to this beach destination located in a sleepy village. According to Baxter, "Going to Bawley Point is the quintessential summer family holiday, with the pulsing surf, hot sand between the toes and the feeling of flying back to shore in the foam of a crashing wave."[18]

That might not be stimulating enough for thirteen-year-old Maya Burton, who cites another New South Wales spot as her desired destination. "The Bottle House Mining Museum in Lightning Ridge is amazing and most of the shops were based on opals," she said. "The miner's cottage, built in 1916, was memorable and I thought the cactus farm was incredible, as was going into different mines so far down into the earth they were like another world. One even had its own art gallery sculptured into the wall."[19]

El Questro in Kimberley is located on the opposite corner of Australia from New South Wales. And it certainly excited fifteen-year-old Erin Park, who endured a long, bumpy ride on rough roads to get to the resort. "The camping ground was right on the beautiful Pentecost River," she explains. "Hot showers and a laundry were a welcome bonus to wash off the red dust, but even better were the natural hot baths at Zedebee Thermal Springs. There are waterfalls and canyons to explore and there's even a mini-township that has a store and steakhouse restaurant."[20]

The memories of each destination serve as lifetime treasures for Australian teenagers. But most important in the moment are the emotional connections gained between themselves and their families. Given the stresses of daily life, such vacations are valued by all involved. One parent wrote the following after a trip to the Gold Coast in Queensland: "When your 15-year-old says it's about family bonding, something must be going right."[21]

CHAPTER THREE

School and Beyond

On August 14, 2017, around 2:30 in the morning, a loud cheer erupted in the library of Doonside Technology High School in western Sydney. Students at the school had been working for months on a science project aimed at improving space travel. They were cheering the successful Florida launch of a commercial SpaceX rocket headed for the International Space Station. Aboard that rocket was their project, which included a series of measurements aimed at determining how the human body reacts to ultraviolet radiation, air pressure, light intensity, and other aspects of space travel. The SpaceX rocket also carried experiments from six other Australian schools. Doonside year-eight student Harrison Tri, one of forty-five students in years seven to eleven who designed the school's experiments, was ecstatic at the sight of the SpaceX rocket soaring skyward. "It was very exciting to watch it live, to actually see the rocket launch almost makes you feel like you're there watching it even though it's on the other side of the world,"[22] Tri said.

> "Our conclusions could help scientists and astronauts in the future create many things which may even save lives one day."[23]
>
> —Harrison Tri, year-eight student at Doonside Technology High School

Information gathered by space station scientists for the student experiments was to be returned to Earth, so that the students could analyze the data and report their findings. Reflecting on the potential benefits of their work, Tri added, "Our conclusions could help scientists and astronauts in the future create many things which may even save lives one day."[23]

This program is an example of recent efforts to increase student engagement in the science and technology needs of the future.

The Australian government has committed more than $12 million to increasing science, technology, engineering, and math teaching in the nation's schools—beginning with primary school education.

School Basics

School is mandatory for all Australian students between the ages of six and fifteen (sixteen in Tasmania). Many kids learn to adapt to time away from their parents in preschools and day care centers before beginning kindergarten, which is the first stage of schooling in Australia but is not required. Compulsory formal education starts the first year of primary school and continues for six or seven years. Students generally then move on to secondary school, though some systems offer middle school in years five and six.

About two-thirds of all Australian students attend free public schools. Other students opt for private schools or are homeschooled by parents or a tutor. The school year generally starts in late January and ends just before Christmas. Vacations run for five to six weeks in between, and students also get two weeks off between the four annual school terms. The school day starts between 8 and 9 a.m. and concludes between 3 and 4 p.m. Students receive a morning break and, in some schools, an afternoon break. Most schools offer early-morning and late-afternoon care for students of working parents.

Australian students at all levels are offered a well-rounded curriculum that includes English, math, history, science, social studies, and health. However, students who wish to take electives such as art and music mostly are out of luck. One study revealed that nearly two-thirds of all primary schools in the country do not offer music education.

Teens can also opt to attend vocational schools that provide more specific training in agriculture and technical skills. They are most often geared toward students who do not plan to further their education at the university level. Vocational training is delivered within the broader curriculum. It allows secondary students to plan for real-world jobs and gain workplace experience.

Other Aussie students receive their school certificate at the end of year ten. The certificate is usually required to gain employment or an apprenticeship. The year ten certificate can also be a ticket to Technical and Further Education (TAFE) courses. These courses are designed to expedite students' entry into the job market upon graduation. The course offerings are wide-ranging. For instance, the TAFE schools in New South Wales offer about twelve hundred courses that can help students forge careers in many different fields. Among the most popular courses are those in nursing, building trades, hospitality, information technology, children's services, cookery and wine, and animal care. TAFE courses have proven attractive to students who cannot afford or do not want a university education.

A SpaceX Falcon 9 rocket heads into space to rendezvous with the International Space Station. Students at several Australian high schools cheered its 2017 launch because their school projects were aboard.

Dropping Out of School

A 2015 study showed that about one-fourth of all Australian students drop out before completing high school. The percentage is much higher among those living in remote and economically disadvantaged communities. The problem is most acute in the Northern Territory and Tasmania, where just over half of all students graduate. Research shows that only about 60 percent of students from low socioeconomic backgrounds complete their high school educations compared to about 90 percent of their wealthier peers.

Among the dropouts is sixteen-year-old Anna, who left her school in Victoria because she lacked direction. She blames her own lack of direction as well as too little help from the school. "I just couldn't do it anymore, being at a mainstream school, it

School Uniforms

For years Australian schools have required students to wear uniforms. Uniforms were thought to instill a sense of discipline and conformity, but they have come under criticism in recent years. Students have complained that wearing identical clothes and, in some cases, even being told how to style their hair has weakened their individuality and potential for self-expression. Sofia Myhre, an eleven-year-old student from Perth, had another reason for wanting to dump her skirt uniforms: they restricted her movement, making it difficult to thrive in school activities such as soccer and netball or do handstands at recess. Her brothers had been allowed to wear shorts and pants throughout primary school. She wanted the same freedom.

So Myhre did something about it in September 2017. She registered a complaint to the Western Australia Education Department (WAED). She was not alone in her dissatisfaction. A group called the Girls' Uniform Agenda had been campaigning for girls to be given the option of wearing shorts and pants. Their efforts finally paid off when the WAED announced in 2017 that it would change the statewide dress code to offer girls more options. Myhre was thrilled. "I think she yelped in joy actually and jumped up and down," her mother said. "She was really excited."

Isabella Kwai, "Girls in Western Australia Gain Right to Wear Pants and Shorts to School," *New York Times*, September 11, 2017. www.nytimes.com.

was getting too hard, it wasn't the help I needed and whatnot. It was more because I was still too young and I had no idea where I wanted to go in any pathways or future-wise and I needed that extra help." Her story, however, has a happy ending. Anna worked as a supermarket cashier before realizing after a year that she needed to finish school. At age nineteen, she enrolled in a school that specializes in educating dropouts. "I've gotten the help," she reports. "I feel better about myself. . . . It's something that I really do need. I've got the pathways open and honestly I just couldn't be happier now."[24]

Rural Learning

The drop-out rate in rural and remote areas of Australia is also a concern. Alcoholism and poverty contribute to the difficulties faced by students of Aboriginal and Torres Strait Islander descent. Terazita, a sixteen-year-old Aboriginal student who grew up in Alice Springs (a Northern Territory town in a remote area in central Australia) and later moved away, was interviewed for a documentary titled *Insight*. In the documentary she describes how difficult it was to concentrate on her studies in the environment of that small town. Fights in Alice Springs were commonplace—and she was involved in many of them. Residents young and old got drunk often, leading to violence at home and in the streets. It is a place where dreams can die. But Terazita would not let that happen. "I don't think Alice Springs . . . is a good environment for me to study and to focus on my education to finish school," she says. "You get a lot of peer pressure and family violence sometimes, back with the community where I used to live at. There used to be a lot of fights and it was like everywhere you go . . . and all to do with alcohol. I remember it was scary."[25]

Terazita learned that fighting back mentally and emotionally was far more productive than fighting back physically. She refused to allow her circumstances to determine her future. She dreamed of joining the navy and making her family proud. She worked toward that goal and urged other Aboriginal youth to battle through adversity. "Don't let anyone hold you back and tell you [that] you can't do it because at the end of the day, it's not another person telling you to do something. It's yourself and you have to be self-motivated."[26]

Most students in the outback do all their schooling remotely through distance education programs, which offer a wide range of subjects online. Upon entering years eleven and twelve, students must select courses that will be continued until graduation. That enables outback students to complete a certificate or start an apprenticeship while still in school.

The comparatively tiny rural student population in Australia translates into comparatively tiny schools. Some are so small that they require just one or two teachers on staff and entire student bodies merged into a single room. This setup has not translated into a better education for rural students. Studies have shown that rural students are 1.5 years behind their urban counterparts in English and math skills, are less likely to complete year twelve, and are half as likely to attend college. In an April 2017 report, the Australian Association for Research in Education expressed concern about those differences and about the mindset of many rural students toward school. According to the report,

> Rural students often say that year 12, or university, are not relevant to their lives and future work, and they would have to leave town to complete them anyway. Communities also express concern because students that leave often don't come back. . . . How will increasing the rate of participation in higher education help our students and their rural communities? . . . The traditional perception of rural education is one of disadvantage. It is seen as something that needs improving. This is because school achievement, completion and access to further study are always measured in relation to the city. The aim seems to be to have no major differences in the results of city children and country children.[27]

Rural students are not alone in placing little importance on year twelve. Some students in urban and suburban schools feel the same way. But many others in high schools around the country feel a heavy burden upon them once their last year of high school rolls around.

Sweating Out Year Twelve

The last year of high school, called year twelve, can be stressful. Some students are under a lot of pressure—either self-imposed or placed on them by parents—to perform at a certain level. In 2016 filmmaker Laura Waters provided cameras to a diverse group of eighteen-year-olds throughout Australia so they could document their experiences in school and beyond. Their final year of high school proved to be an ideal time to extract their thoughts and feelings. They were expressed in the documentary *My Year 12 Life*, which aired on Australian television in February 2017.

Year twelve is when students take their high school certification exams, which determine their Australian Tertiary Admission Rank. This measure of academic achievement is used by universities to select students for undergraduate course work. It is no wonder that many Aussies in year twelve feel their entire futures are on the line.

Students attend a class in the lecture halls of the University of Technology in Sydney. About half of the country's high-school graduates go on to pursue higher education.

The students featured in *My Year 12 Life* seemed unafraid to share their fears and admit to the enormous pressures they felt both academically and personally. Although their attitudes about the importance of education varied, they all expressed concern about how the burden of school impacted their present and future, their relationships, their self-esteem, and their lifestyles. One unnamed teenager expressed her fears just three days before embarking on year twelve. She showed how confused she was about her own feelings. "How messed up is it how much I'm dreading going to school? I should be excited to go back because I'm going to learn all these incredible things. But, no, I'm nervous and I'm worried and I'm scared of failure,"[28] she said.

In the documentary, one high school senior tried unsuccessfully to hold back her tears as she spoke about the anger and stress she was experiencing. Her emotions were on full display as she faced the camera and talked about herself, but she was also expressing the same feelings that trouble many of her peers. She had decided to fight back against the notion of being defined by her performance in the classroom:

> I am feeling so much pressure and I'm feeling so much stress and expectations to do the best I can. And I can't. I can't. I can't. I'm not Superman. I'm at the point where I'm ready to turn around and rebel against it all and say, "Look,

Falling Behind

Australian students have fallen behind their counterparts from other countries academically, according to the Programme for International Student Assessment survey. The survey, published in 2015, showed a significant drop in the reading, math, and science skills of Australian fifteen-year-olds since 2000 while those of other nations had improved. The survey also revealed that the same Australian students were 3 years behind students of the same age in Shanghai, China, in math and 1.5 years behind in reading. The report noted that the average Australian fifteen-year-old had the same problem-solving abilities as a typical twelve-year-old pupil from South Korea.

> you can shove . . . school." . . . Because I don't want to do any of it. Because I'm not going to let a number on a piece of paper—four letters and a number on a piece of paper—at the end of it all tell me what I can and can't be.[29]

One student that sweated it out and survived was Zoe Mallett, who received good grades at her all-girls school in Victoria. It required a lot more than hard work. She was battling a complicated family situation and a roller coaster relationship. Even after the traumatic experiences had ended, Mallett wondered if it had all been worthwhile. "I honestly am not sure if it was worth it," Mallett told the world in the documentary *My Year 12 Life*. "On one hand it was worth it, because I came out the other side and I'm a lot stronger and a lot wiser and I know myself a lot better, and I did get good marks. It's not like anything went to waste. But on the other hand, I struggled a lot mentally, and it was the worst year of my life. On that side of things, I think is it really worth it to go through that much stress?"[30]

> **"I am feeling so much pressure and I'm feeling so much stress and expectations to do the best I can. And I can't. I can't. I can't. I'm not Superman."[29]**
>
> —A high school senior on her anxieties over school

Starting with a Good Attitude

Not all students experience the same level of stress. Ben Kenworthy, who attends an all-boys Catholic school in Victoria, tried to enjoy his last year in high school. A self-proclaimed class clown, Kenworthy refused to allow himself to be overwhelmed. The result was a carefree year twelve:

> Definitely worth it, it was a terrific year. . . . All the pressures, stresses, exams, and tests, they were all definitely worthwhile, without a doubt. Just being around your good mates, just all days, five days a week . . . that's something special. . . .
>
> I didn't really find it too stressful because I try not to stress. I see it as something bad. Obviously, there's times you don't feel great or feel a bit anxious, but I tried my best not

> to stress and keep a cool head, so it was pretty good on the whole. I remember a few people would come to you saying, "Year 12 is the best year of your life." So I went into it at the start of the year with that in mind. Looking back, for sure, it was one of the best years of my life.[31]

Kenworthy is a bit of an exception. One global study of student welfare concluded that Australian teenagers are the most stressed out in the world. They feel greater pressure to succeed than their counterparts in other countries. Queries revealed that half of Aussie boys and three-fourths of Aussie girls admit to feeling stress over their schoolwork. Nearly 90 percent of fifteen-year-olds stated a desire to get top marks in most subjects, and more than 60 percent reported that they are tutored for an average of 4.5 hours a week. Some do not even have time for proper nutrition. About 25 percent of the fifteen-year-olds interviewed said they eat no breakfast before heading off to school.

The Next Level of Education

About half of all Australian students attend universities. Those who attended private secondary schools are the most likely to further their educations. More than 67 percent go on to college, a percentage that has continued to rise. By comparison, 45 percent of public school students attended college in 2016. That statistic represents a slight drop from the previous two years.

Family income greatly determines who attends college in Australia. Students from the poorest regions of Australia account for only 16 percent of the total number of college students. That figure represents only a tiny increase in recent years. The indigenous population is particularly underrepresented. In 2014 just 1.4 percent of all university students in Australia came from indigenous backgrounds.

The relative dominance of female college students is striking. They have outnumbered their male counterparts since 1987. There were just eighty males for every one hundred females in Australian universities in 2014. Yet despite the higher numbers of women on college campuses, studies have shown they have lower income expectations. Women are underrepresented in such fields of study as engineering and related technologies as well as architecture and building. Males are less likely to pursue careers in education, health, and the creative arts.

Recent studies have shown that what matters most to many young Australians of both genders is professional fulfillment without the anxiety that has plagued their educations. Deciding on a career path alone causes enough stress.

The Trend Toward Less Traditional Jobs

Top career prospects for 2017 in Australia included health care, technology, and the building and construction sectors, according to the job search website Indeed. This list was based on job postings, salaries, and opportunities for growth statistics. The company identified marketing manager—especially digital marketing—as the best job in Australia for that year. Chris McDonald, Indeed's managing director for Australia and New Zealand, also notes that young Australians are not motivated solely by money. "Today's work force isn't just looking for a competitive salary and benefits

Health care is a booming industry in Australia. The field is one of the top prospects for employment in Australia, and its high-paying job opportunities make it attractive for young people.

package. People also want job satisfaction, culture fit, a positive work environment and career growth opportunities,"[32] he says.

The career goals of Australian teens run the gamut from practical to dreamlike. But one study showed that the percentage of young people motivated to create their own businesses or driven by personal passion rather than materialism and financial wealth is significant. They were also more inspired by rewarding careers that provide flexibility in their personal lives.

> "Today's work force isn't just looking for a competitive salary and benefits package. People also want job satisfaction, culture fit, a positive work environment and career growth opportunities."[32]
>
> —Chris McDonald, Indeed's managing director for Australia and New Zealand

The Australian Institute of Families reported in 2017 that, though 60 percent of fifteen-year-olds surveyed sought professional or managerial jobs, many others dreamed of taking their creative and athletic talents to the highest levels. Fortune was not a strong motivator, but the same could not be said about fame. The survey showed that very few teens planned to seek out less prestigious jobs such as in retail, hospitality, and manufacturing. But more than 1 in 10 preferred so-called glamorous or fantasy jobs such as professional soccer (called *football* in Australia) player, actor, ballet dancer, YouTuber, and even "Apple genius."[33]

The anything-goes mindset of Australian teens is evident in fifteen-year-old Michael Pupko, a student at McKinnon Secondary College in Melbourne. He expresses a yearning to start his own business and notes that there "is a lot more variety in the job market"[34] than there once was. That Australian fifteen-year-olds are aware of trends in the job market represents a change from past generations. Evie Dinkelmeyer, a classmate of Pupko's at McKinnon, understands what is happening in her desired profession. She yearns to be a journalist. "It's kind of worrying with the decline of newspapers, but I know it will be OK with the move to digital,"[35] she says.

The wide variety of professional aspirations that do not focus on materialistic goals reflects the motivations of many Australian teenagers. They place personal fulfillment, maximizing creativity, and the freedom associated with running their own business ahead of what they perceive as the more mundane lifestyle of 9-to-5 employment and answering to a boss.

CHAPTER FOUR

Being Social

Teresa studies dance in her spare time. But when the sixteen-year-old suburban Australian is not in school or twirling around the floor, she is often browsing the web or connecting with friends and acquaintances on social media. And, like a lot of other teens, Teresa finds herself wishing for a more exciting life when she sees the social media posts of others. "I always compare myself to other people . . . and think, 'Wow, why can't I be like that?'" she says. "When I look at stuff online I see lots of pressures from other people to do what they're doing and be like them. But then I have to calm myself down and think, 'wait, I'm unique. I'm myself.'"[36]

Spending Time Online

Like teens in many other countries, Australian teens live in a world steeped in online surfing, video streaming, and social media. Research published in 2016 reveals that 91 percent of Australian teens between the ages of fourteen and seventeen have a cell phone—and nearly all of those teens (94 percent) have smartphones. Younger Australians are not far behind. The same research shows that more than 50 percent of twelve-year-olds and 75 percent of thirteen-year-olds also have cell phones. Additionally, those fourteen- to seventeen-year-olds are twice as likely as cell phone users of other age groups to use their phones to play music, videos, and games. Almost half claim they cannot live without one.

Whether using a cell phone or computer, Australian teens and young adults spend a lot of time online. A 2016 snapshot of online behavior by Australian teens reveals that 83 percent of fourteen- to seventeen-year-olds and 90 percent of eighteen- to twenty-four-year-olds go online three or more times a day. And cell phones are "the single biggest factor in teens spending increased hours online,"[37] according to research published by the Australian Communications and Media Authority (ACMA) and the Office of the Children's eSafety Commissioner.

Among Australian teens and young adults, one of the most popular online activities is engaging with friends, acquaintances, and others on social media. The authors of "The State of Australian Social Media in 2017" write that social media's influence on young people is "undeniable." They continue: "Almost every Australian aged between 18 and 29 is on social media (99 per cent). Unsurprisingly, it's this younger demographic who are the highest users: 89 per cent will check their favourite networks at least once per day."[38]

All of this online activity is a normal and integral part of life for Australia's teens. It is how they keep in touch with friends, how they explore the world beyond their own neighborhoods, and

Australian teens are plugged into the Internet through cell phones. They spend a good portion of their days on their phones surfing the Web, interacting on social media, playing music and games, and texting friends.

how they have fun. The online habits of Australian teens are also, at times, the cause of social anxiety. This is true for twelve-year-old Olivia, who lives in one of Australia's wealthy suburban communities. Olivia had been bullied and miserable at school, but one would not know it based on what she posts on Instagram and other social media sites. What she posts and what she feels are two entirely different things. "There's, like, Instagram, Snapchat, Twitter, You Tube, et cetera," she says.

> There's not really a winner but it's a competition in a way to [get] the most followers on Instagram. And you've got to have the perfect picture. You do feel like it really does have to be perfect. It really does have to look like you're living this perfect life and everything in your life is perfect and you haven't got a worry. Everything's cute and happy and there's nothing really wrong. When, in reality, there is, but you don't want people to know that.[39]

The use of cell phones and the immersion in the world of social media represent two big differences between today's young Australians and the Australians of previous generations. There are also other signs that the country's youth population is going its own way.

Rejecting the Drinking Culture

One of these changes involves the traditional drinking culture of generations past. To a great extent, this tradition has been rejected by Australia's modern young people. Among them are Lachlan Lewis and his girlfriend, Stephanie Russo. These twenty-year-old students who recently moved to Sydney have discovered that Australia's biggest city is quite expensive. They must spend wisely. So, they do not buy alcohol despite being older than the legal drinking age of eighteen. And that is fine with Lewis. He plays the rugged sport of rugby and must stay sharp. "It's smarter not to drink," he says. "I play better if I don't. Drinking a lot is just not the lifestyle either of us lead. We are paying rent, we're both studying, we just can't afford to go out like that anymore."[40]

They are not alone. A 2016 Australian Institute of Health and Welfare report revealed that only about one in four Australian

Good News for Gamers

Any Australian student who has been told by a parent or teacher that playing online video games is a waste of time could reply with the results of recent research from the Royal Melbourne Institute of Technology (RMIT). That research showed that scores in math, reading, and science were higher among gamers than those who spent time on social media sites. RMIT professor Alberto Posso explains why: "Students who play online games almost every day score 15 points above the average student in maths and 17 points above the average in science. When you play online games, you're solving puzzles to move to the next level and that involves using some of the general knowledge and skills in maths, reading, and science, that you've been taught during the day." Posso suggests that teachers should consider incorporating nonviolent video games into their lessons. That is one teaching tool many students would probably not complain about.

Rae Johnston, "Australian Study Finds Playing Video Games Improves School Grades," Gizmodo, August 9, 2016. www.gizmodo.com.au.

teenagers drink alcohol. The figure has tumbled from 56 percent to 28 percent in just one decade. Those who partake in risky drinking—more than four drinks in one session—dropped from 17 percent in 2004 to less than 9 percent in 2013. And those who participate in binge drinking, which is more than eleven drinks in one sitting, fell from 11 percent to 6 percent.

The shrinking numbers represent a rebellion of sorts against what has been a traditional drinking culture in Australia. Steve Allsop, an alcohol expert with the National Drug Research Institute, states that modern teens have rejected that image for many reasons, including health and money. "There is a generational thing where teenagers don't want to be like their parents," Allsop says about the new data. "Some young people have been affected by images of drunkenness and violence, and they don't want to be in that space. . . . More teenagers have become aware of the health consequences, and sport is really important to them."[41]

Dating, Relationships, and Sex

There are no formal rules in Australia when it comes to dating. Probably the most common scenario is a group of friends gathering for a movie or an evening at the beach. Couples generally do not go out on their own until after they are in a relationship. Even then, it is not uncommon for a couple to invite several single friends to join them for a night out. Who pays for dinner or a movie is sometimes determined by who initiated the night out. But Australian young people are used to everyone paying their share of the bill—whether they are on a couples date or having a night out with a group of friends.

Australia's teens try to make good choices when it comes to relationships and sex. Overall, the country's young people act responsibly and feel good about their decisions regarding having or not having sex. That is the conclusion of the most recent National Survey of Australian Secondary Students and Sexual Health. The survey studied the sexual behavior, attitudes, and health of more than two thousand secondary students in schools across the country. What it found is that many secondary students are sexually active, but at none of those grade levels were the majority of students having sex. In year ten, about one-fourth of students said they were having sex. In year eleven, that number was about one-third. In year twelve, that number was about one-half. Additionally, when asked about condom use, 86 percent of teenagers said they had used a condom the last time they had sex. Researchers also asked teen survey participants who had not had sexual intercourse to describe their feelings in connection with this choice. "[Fifty percent] of those who had not had intercourse felt good about this decision, with religion, culture and pressure from parents being less important than personal decision making,"[42] the survey found.

> "[Fifty percent] of those who had not had intercourse felt good about this decision, with religion, culture and pressure from parents being less important than personal decision making."[42]
>
> —National Survey of Australian Secondary Students and Sexual Health

Not all of Australia's teens and young adults are involved in opposite-sex relationships. Recent studies show an increase in teens and young adults who identify as homosexual.

One such study found that 5 percent of fourteen- to nineteen-year-olds identified as homosexual in 2012 to 2014 (up from 3 percent in 2006 to 2008). Among Australians in their twenties, 7 percent described themselves as homosexual in 2012 to 2014, compared to 4 percent in 2006 to 2008. The report's author suggests a possible explanation: "The rising rate across all age groups shows that people who consider themselves homosexual are becoming more open about it, which reflects increasing acceptance across society."[43]

Another societal change is the use of social media in connection with sex and sexuality. In the national survey, students were asked about the recent phenomenon of sexting, or sending explicit photos via smartphone. Sexting has become prevalent in dating and sexual behavior among Australia's teens. Fifty-four percent of survey participants said they had received a sexually explicit text message, and 26 percent said they had sent a sexually explicit photo of themselves. The numbers rose dramatically among those who were sexually active. In this group, 84 percent said they had received a sexually explicit text, and 72 percent said they had sent one.

> "I notice that girls just think of guys as sex objects and they just want to be with them because of their masculinity and their body type. They don't feel any real love for them. They just want them for their body."[44]
>
> —Fourteen-year-old Dylan

While many of Australia's young people enjoy healthy opposite-sex and same-sex relationships, some struggle to understand their own feelings as well as the feelings of others. Fourteen-year-old Dylan enjoys playing online video games with his friends from his home in Melbourne. But the games and the competition are not the only attractions. The relaxed atmosphere allows him to express his feelings about personal issues. One topic that often arises among both girls and boys is the superficiality of relationships. "I notice that girls just think of guys as sex objects and they just want to be with them because of their masculinity and their body type," Dylan says. "They don't feel any real love for them. They just want them for their body."[44]

Sixteen-year-old Gabrielle, who lives in one of Australia's suburban neighborhoods, voices a virtually identical complaint to that of Dylan. She believes girls are judged more for their bodies than

A young Australian couple skateboards along an oceanfront walkway. The country's young people generally believe they act responsibly in their relationship choices, including their decisions to practice safe sex.

for their brains. "I know there's some boys that do think that all the girls are just kind of like sex toys, which is horrible. And they then go to parties and treat girls like that and that's where you have to be careful."[45]

Sand and Surf

One way that Australian teens can escape the pressures of social relationships (and school) is by heading to the beach, which is quite a short drive for many. Australian Instagram sensation Alex Hayes encapsulated what meeting and playing on the beach means to the teens of his country in just eight words: "Beach culture, Australia, Australians," he said. "Just cruising through life."[46] Indeed, the beach is a place where worries melt away and mindless fun replaces the anxieties associated with school and work. Surfing and swimming in the warm water refreshingly soaks away the stresses for Aussie teens from the east coast to the west coast.

Beaches are a gathering place for Aussie teens on any warm, sunny afternoon, but they are particularly attractive for events such as rock concerts and surfing competitions. Yet one need not boast a high skill level to enjoy surfing at one of Australia's many beaches. Kids with a distinct lack of talent enjoy the challenge whether hanging out with friends or surfing by themselves.

In a 2015 interview, amateur surfers Douglas and Anna talked about their love of Manly Beach near Sydney. Douglas is a native of Brazil, and Anna is from Switzerland. They both came to Manly

Young Australians often spend time at the beach. A large number partake in one of the country's favorite pastimes—surfing. Bondi Beach, pictured here, is a popular spot near Sydney that draws surfers from near and far.

Beach to take English-language courses through an international study abroad program. Their school's campus is just a stone's throw from the beach. Douglas spoke about how he embraced the opportunity to exercise and relax. Surfing, he added, gave him peace. Anna also expressed her fond feelings of Manly. "I started surfing here a few days after my arrival," she reported. "I love being so near the sea and the city at the same time."[47]

A Focus on Sports

Surfing is just one of the many sports enjoyed by Australian youth. Swimming is another. Recent studies show that 48.8 percent of kids ages six to thirteen regularly swim. The most popular team sport for kids in that same age group is soccer. These same studies show that 48.7 percent of young Aussies play soccer. Other popular youth sports include cycling, track and field, basketball, dancing, cricket, netball, and tennis. Among youth ages fourteen and older, the most popular sports are swimming and cycling.

Dancing, considered a sport in Australia, is popular with both little kids and teens. The face of sixteen-year-old suburbanite Gabrielle lit up when asked about dancing in an interview for the 2015 documentary *Our Kids: Why Are They So Stressed?* She did not look stressed at all when speaking about her favorite activity. "I've been dancing since I was two-years-old," she said. "And I've never stopped and I've loved every single minute of it."[48] Fellow sixteen-year-old dancer Claudia expressed similar sentiments. "When I dance, I feel like I can fly," she said. "It's amazing."[49] Seventeen-year-old Emily, who shares the dance floor with Gabrielle and Claudia, also gets great enjoyment out of dancing. "It's a place where I can be free and happy with all my friends; we're like a big family. And we support each other, we encourage each other through everything and it allows me to relieve stress from any family or school pressures I have."[50]

"It's a place where I can be free and happy with all my friends; we're like a big family. And we support each other, we encourage each other through everything and it allows me to relieve stress from any family or school pressures I have."[50]

—Seventeen-year-old Emily on dancing

Losing That Competitive Spirit

Young Australians are participating less in competitive sports than they once did. According to Roy Morgan Research, males ages fourteen to twenty-four remain the most likely to partake in such activities, but their numbers have fallen from 57 percent in 2001 to just 42 percent in 2016. The rate among females dropped from 38 percent to 33 percent during the same period. The sports that suffered the largest drop in participation among all Australians were squash, tennis, golf, and netball. Rowing, soccer, and badminton made the greatest gains.

The decreasing participation in tennis is particularly discouraging to traditionalists. Australia has produced many of the greatest tennis players in history. The Australian Open, played annually in January, is one of four main competitions on the professional tour.

Playing youth sports also fuels dreams of competing on the professional level. Such dreams run rampant on the soccer fields of suburban Sydney, where twelve-year-old Cameron hones his skills. He lists soccer as one of the three biggest concerns in his life. His stated goal is to play someday for British soccer powerhouse Manchester United. Few young people will ever play professional sports, but dreaming is motivational. And the ability to motivate oneself is one virtue that kids can carry with them forever.

The Gaming Culture

Not all activities embraced by Australian youth plant the seeds for future success. Some, such as gaming, are simply fun and provide a diversion from the cares of the day. Fourteen-year-old Dylan, who lives in a middle-class Australian neighborhood, looked embarrassed when asked if he was supposed to be playing the video game he was playing. After all, it was the ultraviolent *Call of Duty*, which requires its players to shoot to kill. Dylan's mother was not supposed to know, but the inclusion of his interview on the *Our Kids* documentary likely served as a confession. Though he understood his mother's protests, he did not believe he should back down either. The issue was not about the game itself. It was about the social interaction revolving around the game. "My mom is quite protective on what games I play," Dylan said. "She doesn't like the idea of killing people or violence for entertainment. I'm quite annoyed."[51]

Dylan and his buddies have grown up in an era of sophisticated games that can be played on a variety of devices. A study released in 2016 showed that 90 percent of Australians ages five to fourteen consider themselves video game players, the highest percentage of all age groups. The same study found that 84 percent of Australians between the ages of fifteen and twenty-four are gamers. That group listed relieving boredom and having fun as their two primary reasons for gaming.

Like the youth populations of many other countries, Australia's young people enjoy connecting with friends—both in person and through social media. They are actively engaged in sports, and many find pleasure spending time in front of their consoles and computers playing video games. These and other activities provide important social outlets for relieving stress and, just as importantly, for enjoying and engaging with the world around them.

CHAPTER FIVE

Developing a Worldview

Alisha could not avoid all the bad news even if she wanted to. It is everywhere. She is bombarded with stories about terrorism, homelessness, starvation, war, racism, and dozens of other issues. They all prey on the mind of the eighteen-year-old. She understands that solving such enormous problems will eventually fall to her generation. To Australians her age, these issues seem overwhelming. And that makes her depressed. "You turn on the news and it's all this horrible stuff happening and you go on Facebook and there are stories of suicide and car crashes and everywhere you look there seems to be so much despair and I think there's a lot of pressure put on our generation, that we need to fix the world," Alisha says. "I'd watch the news and I'd look at these starving children and I'd look at the state of the economy and I'd look at the mess the world was in and I would sort of feel like I had to change all of this and I feel so alone in doing that."[52]

In her more hopeful moments, Alisha realizes that she is not alone and that she can make a difference. Aussie teens who will inherit the problems created by previous generations have in general developed a worldview that is less conservative and is more socially tolerant and politically liberal. And they intend to make a difference.

Thinking About the World

Social research specialist Maggie Hamilton, who focuses on childhood development, understands the fears felt by Australian youth. They are like those who see a raging fire but have neither the expertise nor the resources to put it out. "There's a very clear sense that they're about to be handed a poison chalice," Hamilton says. "And that's because of the massive amount of news that we have now—the 24-hour cycle where they see environmental degradation, we see ISIS, we see the flux of migrants. And so they're left in that place of pain and bewilderment and these issues being much larger than what they can personally deal with."[53]

> "You turn on the news and it's all this horrible stuff happening and you go on Facebook and there are stories of suicide and car crashes and everywhere you look there seems to be so much despair and I think there's a lot of pressure put on our generation, that we need to fix the world."[52]
>
> —Eighteen-year-old Alisha

Even preteens in Australia feel the pain others suffer around the world. They could selfishly think only about themselves and try to shut off their empathy. But the news is all around them in the age of social media and the Internet. That makes it harder to be self-centered. And the kids understand that a concern about global issues, as well as domestic issues involving their fellow Australians, is a necessity. They understand that the weight of the world's problems will eventually fall to their generation to solve.

Among the young Australians that have become aware of current events is twelve-year-old Zach. In a simpler world, most kids his age would concern themselves with family, school, and how many goals they could score in their next soccer match. But Zach freely admits his concerns about larger world issues. "I worry about some things like terrorism, racism, and poverty around the world, and some diseases,"[54] he says.

Young Australians, according to two recent polls, are less interested in traditional politics than older Australians. However, researchers say, they are engaged with issues such as climate change, same-sex marriage, housing affordability, and education—issues that have risen to prominence during their upbringing. Their way of addressing issues like these also differs from older generations. Rather than working through established political parties, researcher Max Halupka notes, young people are becoming active "in ways that generations of Australians were not engaged: signing online petitions, being vocal on social media, blogging and supporting online campaigns."[55]

The King River on the island of Tasmania has suffered pollution from nearby mines. Young people in Australia are aware of these threats, and most feel that they must support efforts to clean up their surroundings.

Another way many young Australians are making a difference is through volunteer work. The *Mission Australia Youth Survey Report 2016* found that volunteer work is the third most popular activity for young people ages fifteen to nineteen, behind participating in and watching sports. More than half of respondents, 53.5 percent, told researchers that they had done volunteer work during the previous year.

Embracing the Rainbow

Among the issues that resonate with young Australians is equality for the LGBTI community. Engagement with this issue can be seen in one striking photo. Taken during the summer of 2017, it shows a rally of young Australians in favor of legalizing same-sex marriage. At the time, debate over the issue was raging throughout Australia. One of the advocates hoisted a rainbow-colored placard that expressed the feelings of most in her generation. It read, "Love Wins."[56]

Research during that time revealed that 80 percent of Australians ages eighteen to twenty-four favored marriage equality. That statistic reflected the support gay marriage received from most Australian youths. Although it is far from the only social or political issue about which young Aussies have taken a stand for tolerance, it has been one of their most passionate causes. Adam Pulford has been well aware of that for years. A few years back, the Australian youth representative to the United Nations received a group message from students at Hellyer College in the northern Tasmanian town of Burnie. "In an ideal world," they wrote, "people would be equal regardless of sexuality, culture, race, belief, age, ability, or gender. To legalize same-sex marriage would be to set the path of acceptance for the next generation."[57]

> "After I came out, I got loving comments from so many people. And some of the nicest compliments came from people in my hometown. They loved me and embraced me."[58]
>
> —Jake, a rural Australian

That open-mindedness of Australian youth has permeated the country. Gays are far more accepted, even in the more conservative rural areas, than they were not long ago. That pleased a young Australian named Jake. Jake, who is from a small town, wanted to be open about his homosexuality, but he was fearful of how people would react. He soon learned that he had nothing to fear. "I realized that it wasn't my hometown that didn't like me being gay; I didn't like myself for being gay," Jake says. "After I came out, I got loving comments from so many people. And some of the nicest compliments came from people in my hometown. They loved me and embraced me . . . so much so that, whenever I have a bad day, I go back to that Facebook status from [2013] and look at the nice comments to give me a good ol' confidence boost."[58]

At a 2015 rally in Brisbane, young people take a stand for marriage equality and LGBTI rights. Recent studies indicate an overwhelming majority of young adults in Australia favor same-sex marriage.

Superficial vs. Real

Not all of the concerns of Australia's young people are quite so weighty. Many younger Australians are still struggling to figure out what is important in life and what is not. Thirteen-year-old Lilli and twelve-year-old Olivia live in one of the country's wealthy suburban neighborhoods. They attend a private school. They worry about being ostracized if their lifestyles and possessions, such as clothing and accessories, do not live up to other people's expectations. They feel pressure to fit in. "It's like the same thing that would happen 40 years ago—'Oh, you're not wearing that so you're not cool,'" says Lilli. "But now it's escalating to a point where when you have social media you can post pictures about what you're wearing and people pretty much see your outfit for every day of the week. So, it turns out to be something where people are seeing every single aspect of other people's lives."[59]

The result is that shopping at the "right" stores is critical to social success. The threat of being exposed through so-called inferior clothing and accessories is great enough to motivate Lilli and Olivia to shop at more expensive and trendy stores. "At private school, it's almost like a crime to shop at stores like Target, BW, and K-Mart," Olivia says. "You just don't do it. Every now and again, they'll get away with wearing something from a store like Target—you cut off the tags because no one can know."[60]

Though some older teenagers are also prone to pursue superficial goals such as those related to wardrobe, many others have gained a more elevated perspective. They have tried to become more introspective. They are learning ways to find happiness and contentment from within. That has led to a greater openness to new religions and lifestyles. It has also resulted in teens growing less likely to identify with any religion. Though such is not the case with all Australian youths, the trend toward not blindly accepting the religion of one's parents or any religion at all has been strongly established.

The Open Mind

Australia has become a more religiously diverse nation. It has also grown less religious overall. And its youth have fueled the transformation. The change has been dramatic. About 90 percent of Australians identified as Christians in 1966. A steady drop has resulted in just 52 percent claiming that affiliation in 2016. Most significant is that 39 percent of all Australians ages eighteen to thirty-four did not identify with any religion in 2016, and 12 percent identified with religions other than Christianity. Since 2006 Hinduism has been the fastest-growing religion in the country, a statistic driven by Asian immigration. But Buddhism and Islam have also made strong strides.

Several factors have contributed to the weakening of religious belief among young Australians. Among them is its lack of relevance to their lives. Sociologist Andrew Singleton offers that church was once a place for families to socialize and participate in activities, but now youth socialize elsewhere with and without their kin. Young people are simply less likely to participate in any form of organized religion with parents and grandparents.

Many Australian teens and young adults have shied away from religion because they associate it with political and social conservatism. Modern young Aussies tend to take a more liberal outlook on issues such as abortion and gay marriage, both of which have traditionally been viewed negatively by organized religion. Even so, young Australians have not completely closed the door to religion and spirituality.

Trying Something New

Eight students from Byron Bay Public School posed for the camera in December 2016. They sat cross-legged in a meditation position and placed their hands together as if praying. They had been studying Buddhism in class. More than 150 kids in the northern New South Wales school had elected to participate. That represented more than one-fourth of the student population.

And they were far from alone. Schools across New South Wales had been requesting Buddhism scripture teachers and were struggling to keep up with the demand. Students in more than three thousand public schools in that state were studying the religion. The popularity of meditation among young Australians centered on finding inner peace while preventing negative external forces from taking a toll mentally and emotionally. Even students in years two and three gained benefits from the practice.

Brian White is quite aware of the benefits of meditation. He is chairman of the Buddhist Council of New South Wales, which trains the scripture instructors who are so in demand. In an interview, he sought to explain the growing popularity of meditation in Australia. "It's driven by a few things—general raising of awareness in meditation right across society and how beneficial that can be, and the realization that even six and seven-year-olds can

Believers and Nonbelievers

Australian teens and those in their early twenties are less likely to believe in God than those of any other age group in their country, according to research published in 2016. Only 31 percent in that age category answered in the affirmative when asked whether they believe in a supreme being that created the universe. Trends indicate that this percentage will not rise. Studies have shown that only 8 percent of all Australians who once did not believe in God have changed their minds. Though nearly half (47 percent) of Australians still describe themselves as believing in God, their numbers shrink with every generation.

meditate for a few minutes and benefit from that," he said. "But, also, Buddhism itself has a fairly good image across society of being a peaceful and practical way of life."[61]

Although interest in organized religion is falling among Australia's youth population, Christianity and Buddhism still have pretty strong followings. Buddhism has emerged as the second-largest religion in Australia behind Christianity. Studies show that those with parents who attend church regularly are far more likely to identify as Christians. Some maintain their Christian identities into their twenties and beyond.

Taking a Stand

In an effort to increase interest and participation in religious life, religious-based organizations are seeking to understand and take action on the issues critical to young Aussies. On August 20, 2017, more than two hundred young members of a group called Youth PoWR streamed into Santa Sabina College in Strathfield, New South Wales. They had arrived at the Light in Dark Times event. The activities were organized by the Centre for Christian-Muslim Relations. But it brought together those from all religions and even the secular community to discuss racism, discrimination, and climate change. The participants included Jews, Buddhists, Muslims, Christians, Hindus, and Sikhs.

Participants at the event gathered in small groups to discuss a wide range of topics, though climate change and racism emerged as the most passionate for them. They exchanged ideas and discussed actions they could take. Attendees felt a sense of pride at how young Australians representing diverse cultural backgrounds and religions—or no religion at all—could work together on issues about which they felt such passion to achieve a common goal.

Many young Aussies perceive a link between climate change and racism. A proposed coal mine in Queensland attracted hundreds of young people to Melbourne for a protest march in July 2017. The protesters called on their government to place Australia on a path toward 100 percent renewable energy. Young people

With their progressive views, young people will undoubtedly shape Australia's future. They know how to harness the power of social media and are not afraid to speak out.

Staying Away from Cigarettes

Modern Australian teens just might have signaled the early signs of a smoke-free generation. The number of young cigarette smokers has dropped to record lows. In 1996, 77 percent of twelve-to-seventeen-year-olds were smokers; by 2016, however, only 7 percent smoked cigarettes.

Those statistics suggest the effectiveness of antismoking campaigns aimed at youth along with other efforts to reduce smoking. Young Australians are more knowledgeable than ever about the harmful effects of smoking. Other factors in this decline include the establishment of smoke-free areas throughout the country, the monitoring of cigarette sales to minors, and increases in cigarette prices.

representing the SEED Indigenous Youth Climate Network were at the forefront of the demonstration. The Aboriginal and Torres Strait Islander communities have traditionally been most negatively affected by such mining initiatives. Many Australian youths joined them that day to take a stand. Gemma Borgo Caratti, the national director of the Australian Youth Climate Coalition, expressed their sentiments. "Young people are sick of politicians trying to wreck our future," she said. "We'll do whatever we can to oppose that. . . . We know Indigenous people are affected first and worst by this. We need to keep them at the forefront of this action."[62]

> "Young people are sick of politicians trying to wreck our future."[62]
>
> —Gemma Borgo Caratti, the national director of the Australian Youth Climate Coalition

Many Australian youths feel the need to be at the forefront of the action on issues of the day, particularly those dealing with the environment, racism, and LGBTI rights. It remains to be seen how their passion for such issues will translate into positive change. As kids become teens and teens become young adults, they gain a greater understanding that they will soon be making the decisions that could affect their country and the entire world.

SOURCE NOTES

Chapter One: A Unique and Vibrant Land

1. Bill Bryson, "In a Sunburned Country," *New York Times,* 2000. www.nytimes.com.
2. Anthony Horowitz. "Sydney Is the Most Beautiful, Exciting City in the World," *Telegraph* (London), July 7, 2015. www.telegraph.co.uk.
3. Quoted in Jamie Smyth, "Foreign-Born Australians at Record High After Asian-Migrant Surge," *Financial Times,* June 27, 2017. www.ft.com.
4. Quoted in Phil Mercer, "Immigrants Change Australia's Cultural Identity," Voice of America News, June 23, 2012. www.voanews.com.

Chapter Two: Life at Home

5. Quoted in Emma Macdonald and Lara O'Toole, "Today's Teens, a Lot Like Yesterday's," *Sydney Morning Herald,* June 4, 2013. www.smh.com.au.
6. Quoted in Macdonald and O'Toole, "Today's Teens, a Lot Like Yesterday's."
7. Quoted in *Four Corners*, "Our Kids," ABC TV, November 16, 2015. www.abc.net.au.
8. Nicola Harrison. "Is It Unfair to Raise Kids in an Apartment?," Mamamia, April 18, 2012. www.mamamia.com.au.
9. Quoted in Provoke, "Where Small Towns and Teen Life Collide," March 24, 2017. http://provoke.com.au.
10. Quoted in Elders Real Estate Network, "Does Australian Rural Living Make You Happier?," February 13, 2017. www.eldersrealestate.com.au.
11. Child Family Community Australia, "Report—Mental Health in Rural and Remote Communities," June 6, 0217. https://aifs.gov.au.

12. Ninti One Foundation, "Stronger Communities for Children." www.nintione.com.au.
13. Quoted in Shannon Molloy, "Youth Homelessness Is Australia's National Disgrace, with 44,000 Kids Sleeping Rough Right Now," News.com.au. August 3, 2017. www.news.com.au.
14. Quoted in Molloy, "Youth Homelessness Is Australia's National Disgrace, with 44,000 Kids Sleeping Rough Right Now."
15. Pavla Miller and Justin Bowd, "Do Australian Teenagers Contribute to Household Work?," Australian Institute of Family Studies, September 2010. https://aifs.gov.au.
16. Miller and Bowd, "Do Australian Teenagers Contribute to Household Work?"
17. Quoted in TJ Ryan, "Aussie Kids Have to Work to Earn Their Pocket Money," CANSTAR, November 21, 2016. www.canstar.com.au/youth-banking/aussie-kids-work-earn-pocket-money/.
18. Quoted in Fran Molloy, "Whatever to Wicked: Teens' Favourite Destinations," Traveller. www.traveller.com.au.
19. Quoted in Molloy, "Whatever to Wicked."
20. Quoted in Molloy, "Whatever to Wicked."
21. Quoted in Molloy, Whatever to Wicked."

Chapter Three: School and Beyond

22. Quoted in Natasha Robinson, "SpaceX Launch: Australian High School Students Play Major Role in NASA's Resupply Mission," ABC News (Australia), August 14, 2017. www.abc.net.au/news/2017-08-15/spacex-nasa-cargo-launches-student-projects-to-iss/8806524.
23. Quoted in Robinson, "SpaceX Launch."
24. Quoted in Jessica Longbottom, "One in Four Australian Students Drop Out of High School, Study Finds," ABC News (Australia), October 26, 2016. www.abc.net.au.
25. Quoted in Lin Taylor, "Aboriginal Teens Open Up About Life in Alice Springs," Special Broadcasting Service, August 26, 2013. www.sbs.com.au.

26. Quoted in Taylor, "Aboriginal Teens Open Up About Life in Alice Springs."

27. Philip Roberts, "Is Something Going Wrong with Rural and Remote Education in Australia? (Or Is It All About Perception?)," Australian Association for Research in Education, April 10, 2017. www.aare.edu.au.

28. Quoted in ABC TV, "My Year 12 Life: Back to School," YouTube, January 23, 2017. www.youtube.com.

29. Quoted in *Daily Mail* (London), "Girl Highlights Stress About School Results in *My Year 12 Life*," video. www.dailymail.co.uk.

30. Quoted in James Maasdorp, "Is Year 12 Worth It? High School Students Battle Pressures After Self-Documenting Final Year," ABC News (Australia), February 19, 2017. www.abc.net.au.

31. Quoted in Maasdorp, "Is Year 12 Worth It?"

32. Quoted in Chris Pash, "The 20 Best Australian Jobs of 2017," Business Insider Australia, May 30, 2017. www.businessinsider.com.au.

33. Olivia Caisley, "Great Expectations: Teens Want Careers as Actors and You Tubers." *Weekend Australian,* August 15, 2017. www.theaustralian.com.au.

34. Quoted in Caisley, "Great Expectations."

35. Quoted in Caisley, "Great Expectations."

Chapter Four: Being Social

36. Quoted in *Four Corners*, "Our Kids."

37. Australian Communications and Media Authority and the Office of the Children's eSafety Commissioner, "Aussie Teens and Kids Online," *Research Snapshots* (blog), February 5, 2016. www.acma.gov.au.

38. Digital360, "The State of Australian Social Media in 2017," August 3, 2017. http://digital360.com.au.

39. Quoted in *Four Corners*, "Our Kids."

40. Quoted in Natasha Bita, "Teenagers Reject Aussie Drinking Culture, Data Reveals," *Herald Sun* (Melbourne), October 6, 2016. www.heraldsun.com.au.

41. Quoted in Bita, "Teenagers Reject Aussie Drinking Culture, Data Reveals."

42. La Trobe University, "Teen Sexual Health Survey Launched," May 4, 2014. www.latrobe.edu.au.

43. Quoted in Roy Morgan Research, "Is Australia Getting Gayer—and How Gay Will We Get?," June 2, 2015. www.roymorgan.com.

44. Quoted in *Four Corners,* "Our Kids."

45. Quoted in Leesa Smith, "Why Are Our Children So Stressed?," Kidspot Health, November 16, 2015. www.kidspot.com.au.

46. Quoted in Ariel Bogle, "Lifestyles of the Instafamous." Mashable. http://mashable.com.

47. Quoted in Candida, "Australia Open of Surfing: Students Talk About Manly Beach," *Kaplan Experience* (blog), Kaplan International English, February 11, 2015. www.kaplaninternational.com.

48. Quoted in *Four Corners,* "Our Kids."

49. Quoted in *Four Corners,* "Our Kids."

50. Quoted in *Four Corners,* "Our Kids."

51. Quoted in *Four Corners,* "Our Kids."

Chapter Five: Developing a Worldview

52. Quoted in *Four Corners,* "Our Kids."

53. Quoted in *Four Corners,* "Our Kids."

54. Quoted in *Four Corners,* "Our Kids."

55. Quoted in Jason Thomas, "Young Australians Are More Political than We Think, Research Suggests," Special Broadcasting Services News, June 23, 2016. www.sbs.com.au.

56. Quoted in Karen Barlow, "The Massive Drive to Get Students to Enroll for Same-Sex Marriage Vote," August 23, 2017. www.huffingtonpost.com.au.

57. Adam Pulford, "Gay Marriage Is a Vote Changer for Young People," ABC News (Australia), August 19, 2013. www.abc.net.au.

58. Quoted in Reachout.com, "Being Gay in Rural Areas." https://au.reachout.com.
59. Quoted in *Four Corners,* "Our Kids."
60. Quoted in *Four Corners,* "Our Kids."
61. Quoted in Samantha Turnbull, "Buddhism Scripture Teachers Struggling to Keep Up with Demand from State Schools," ABC North Coast, December 14, 2016. www.abc.net.au.
62. Quoted in Sam Langford, "Hundreds of Young People Are Calling for Action on Climate Change in Melbourne's CBD," Junkee, July 24, 2017. http://junkee.com.

FOR FURTHER RESEARCH

Books

Richard Broome, *Aboriginal Australians: A History Since 1788*. Sydney, Australia: Allen & Unwin, 2010.

Peter Hart, *Gallipoli*. New York: Oxford University Press, 2014.

Stella Martin, *Australian Wildlife: Wildlife Explorer*. Chalfont St. Peter, Bucks, England: Bradt Travel Guides, 2010.

Alice Pung, *Growing Up Asian in Australia*. Melbourne, Australia: Black, 2008.

Internet Sources

Natasha Bita and Laura Sullivan, "Australian Schoolkids Top World's Stress List," *Daily Telegraph* (London). April 19, 2017. www.dailytelegraph.com.au/news/nsw/australian-schoolkids-top-worlds-stress-list/news-story/ef29a44322e8f5cf21c8e1fc09f7736b.

The Conversation, "Why Do Schools Want All Students to Look the Same?," April 3, 2017. https://theconversation.com/why-do-schools-want-all-students-to-look-the-same-75611.

Jessica Longbottom, "One in Four Australian Students Drop Out of High School, Study Finds," ABC News (Australia), October 26, 2015. www.abc.net.au/news/2015-10-26/quarter-of-high-school-students-drop-out/6884578.

Pallavi Singhal, "Private School Girls Most Likely to Go to University: Report," *Sydney Morning Herald*, April 16, 2017. www.smh.com.au/national/education/private-school-girls-most-likely-to-go-to-university-report-20170413-gvk6vu.html.

Hanyang Zhao, "Losing My Religion? Why Australian Young People Are Turning Away from God," Online Journalism, April 28, 2016. https://onlinejournalism004.wordpress.com/2016/04/28

/losing-my-religion-why-australian-young-people-are-turning-away-from-god.

Websites

Aboriginal Culture (www.aboriginalculture.com.au). This site provides educational materials on all aspects of modern Aboriginal life in Australia. Included among the subjects are religious and ceremonial traditions, social organizations, and artistic endeavors.

Australian Government: Schools in Australia (www.studyinaustralia.gov.au/english/australian-education/schools). This website presents a thorough examination of the educational system in Australia. It seeks to promote the positive aspects of Australian schools while detailing how students advance through the system and what types of courses they are offered.

Growing Up in Australia: The Longitudinal Study of Australian Children (www.growingupinaustralia.gov.au). This government site details many reports and studies that offer insight into the youth population of Australia. Among the general topics are their social lives and family relationships.

National Geographic Australia (www.nationalgeographic.com/travel/destinations/oceania/Australia). This site explores the physical beauty of Australia. Photos and information about some of the most iconic and breathtaking places in the country are offered here by the National Geographic Society.

INDEX

Note: Boldface page numbers indicate illustrations.

PICTURE CREDITS

Cover: Shutterstock.com/ChameleonsEye

6: Maury Aaseng (map)

6: Shutterstock.com/Julinzy (flag)

7: (top to bottom) Shutterstock.com/Fon Hodes; Shutterstock.com/polygraphus; Shutterstock.com/FS11; Shutterstock.com/GaudiLab

10: Minden Pictures

13: Shutterstock.com/skyearth

17: Aboriginal Men, c.1870 (albumen print), Australian Photographer, (19th century)/Private Collection/ © Michael Graham-Stewart/Bridgeman Images

22: Rafael Ben-Ari/Chameleons Eye/Newscom

27: iStock.com/shells1

31: Shutterstock.com/fritz16

35: Associated Press

39: View Pictures/Richard/VIEW Pictures/Newscom

43: Depositphotos.com/monkeybusiness

46: Shutterstock.com/Syda Productions

51: Shutterstock.com/cktraveling

52: Shutterstock.com/structuresxx

58: Gerald Cubitt/NHPA/Photoshot/Newscom

60: Shutterstock.com/paintings

64: iStock.com/Kokkal Ng

ABOUT THE AUTHOR

Martin Gitlin is a freelance educational book author based in Cleveland, Ohio. He has had more than 120 books published since 2006. Gitlin won more than forty-five awards as a newspaper journalist, including a first-place award for general excellence from the Associated Press in 1996. That organization also selected him as one of the top four feature writers in Ohio in 2001.